A LIFE STORY

By Kris Kuester

A LIFE STORY

Redefined
Published by LWI Publishing, Atlanta, Georgia

ISBN: 978-1449967147

Design by greaterthan> design collective
Published in the United States by
LWI Publishing, Atlanta, Georgia.

Special Sales

This book is available at a special quantity discount when purchased in bulk by corporations, organizations, and other groups. For information please email business@livingwithit.net or call 678-661-1594.

I would like to thank all those who have been apart of this project and Living With It Ministries. My wife, Trudy and daughter, Maddie, who are so willing and supportive of everything we do, we could not do this without you. To my parents, John and Lois, who have supported me all of my days. The LWI board members: Adam Rinehart, Joel Ratekin, Jeff Knock and Kurt Kuester all of you are so willing to give of your wisdom, leadership and guidance to the mission of LWI. Anthony Burns your tireless support and effort for God and all of our projects is beyond measure. To all who remain unmentioned thank you. God thank you for the privilege to serve in this way.

REdefined

Forward - " Living With It"

This is a story that you can't run and hide from. It lives somewhere deep within all of us, the "it." We all have one, and we know it, even though we may not want to admit it. That thing that we wish God would just remove from our life but He just keeps it there to continue the painful process of building our character. Kris's story is life shaping. He has faced his "it" without choice. It's physical, can no longer be hidden, just out there for everyone to see. His ability to transcend through it, I will never forget. I can't explain it. I can't rationalize it. It must be the maker of the universe that makes it possible and it is!

- Dennis Tyson

Chapter 1 - Being Defined

It was hot, really hot. Sweat rolled down my face. I could feel it on my fingers as I tried to re-grip the ball clutched in my hands, tumbling it over and over to get it seated just right. I had been here before. *Just throw it by him, he can't hit you, just throw a strike.* I had to clear my brow to see the catcher's signs. I shook the sign off: *No, not a curve, fastball, that is what is coming.* The crowd cheered for both sides. It was deafening, and this was for everything. You could smell the dirt, the sweat. My heart was beating faster now; I could feel it, and I could almost hear it. *It's now or never what are you going to do?* I wound up and threw the ball as hard as I could. A small grunt came from my mouth, as it flew from my fingertips with everything I had. *Here comes a pipe shot, can you hit it?* The batter picked it up with his eyes, trying to anticipate his swing. Time stood still. You know that slow motion feeling you get right before the clash of two actions intersecting? Ball versus bat, it was out of my hands now. Slow motion quickly turned back to reality and with a dead thud. The ball smashed into the mitt of the catcher; the batter swung as the ball sailed right by him. "Strike three!" yelled the umpire.

It was over. We had won another state championship, my second in that division. I was thirteen; there were maybe a couple hundred people there. For me it might as well have been a big league stadium because that's where I dreamed of being someday. Baseball! Our journey together was just beginning. I was being defined. Defined as an athlete, physically able to do things others couldn't do. It was a feeling I couldn't get enough of - I wanted more, and more is what I got. The words of the great hymn writer John Newton were, "I once was ? but now am ? ." Those are powerful words to me. Newton said, "lost" then "found," but it could be anything: unhappy then happy, in shape now not so much, broken now healed - you get the point. You see what defines you now or then isn't necessarily what needs to define you forever. Which brings up the question, can we really change? Do we morph into something slightly different? What can affect that change? I like to think that we change slightly, more of a morphing, into something different from our former definition. An example: "Bob was a jerk, but you know lately he's been better." Maybe Bob morphed or maybe redefined himself into someone other than his previous definition of "jerk."

Defined

As a kid, my definition was crystal clear: sports. I was raised in a sports family. Six boys and a girl. Maybe you didn't hear that right - six boys and one tough girl! Anne, my sister, was sandwiched between and among six boys; all sports guys to varying degrees. For me, it was everything, all I was interested in, all I wanted do. Our family trips were planned around the next sporting event or season. My dad worked for the federal government, and my mom was a homemaker. It was the '70s. My life was good. I was loved; my early life was much like a *Leave*

It to Beaver episode. I am sure it wasn't quite as simple, but for me it was simple; go to school and then play.

School wasn't my favorite thing. In fact, if I think about it, I hated it and it hated me. My grades were always the topic of discussion in our house; to the contrary my four older brothers were good athletes but also good students. I wasn't. School was boring, I just didn't have a passion for it, unlike sports. Give me a basketball, baseball, or football, and the playing field changed. No longer was it a struggle to get me interested. You had my interest at "Let's play a game" anytime, anywhere as long as it was a sport.

I grew up in the rural stretches of North Dakota. It's cold in North Dakota, real cold, but few realize that it is also very hot in North Dakota. It is a true four-season state. Basketball was in the winter. That didn't stop us, we would play outside in our driveway for hours on end. We would scrape the snow and ice away for just one more game. My dad installed lights on our garage so we could play when it got dark. When it was a really cold day, sometimes the basketball would become hard as a rock, but we played on and the ball barely bounced.

I remember my brother Ryan, who was a great athlete, probably the most talented of the Kuester clan. He would shoot free throws in the dead of winter while I was stuck in the kitchen of our small but comfortable home, doing homework (not fun). The clank of the ball hitting the rim as he kept trying to perfect his free throws was all I heard. These were early lessons but ones that have stuck with me to this day; nothing comes without hard work and persistence. Don't quit; keep trying. Ryan became one of the best free throw shooters in the history of high school basketball in the state of North Dakota. Now, he is a successful computer programmer in California, where he lives with his wife and two children.

I never was the most gifted, but the desire and passion I had for the game of baseball would take me to many places and teach me many lessons. Nobody out-worked me on a practice field, and nobody maximized their minimal talent more than I did. I knew that I had to work harder than everybody to make up for the abilities I didn't have, but little did I know that drive would be so needed later in my life.

Church

My family never missed church when I was growing up; faith has played a huge part of my life from birth. My mother made sure her children were ready to go to church each Sunday. Remember, that was seven kids! Today, I have a five-year-old, and it is a battle to make sure she is ready to go to church. Was my mother jacked up on special mother sauce or what? I couldn't imagine having seven to prep for church, but she did it every Sunday. My dad sang in the choir so it was just my mom, but somehow she did it. Don't think I wasn't watching and somehow processing that; today I'm using those lessons to my advantage.

I found church massively boring, and I wasn't very interested in the whole event. Growing up Lutheran meant a lot of stand up and then sit down, then stand up again, and hey let's throw a kneel in there. It was interesting how God would bring me back to that same place one day. That's right, the same church, to serve the same people in the very place I found to be so boring. In those days I believed God was just a Sunday thing, do it and move on. That would change, too.

Today, I am proud to say that all my siblings and their families are active in their respective churches. I am an ordained pastor, two others are lay pastors, and the rest serve faithfully with their families in their churches.

You see my parents saw a value in something bigger than themselves. That is faith. They wouldn't budge on that principle, and the outcome some thirty years later is striking. Sometimes the harvest takes time, but when it comes it is beautiful.

The Power of Family

I considered my family growing up to be imperfect, full of faults and mistakes, but ultimately

intensely dedicated to each other and their respective needs. Much like a solid team, we've always had each others' backs covered in a faith in each other, as opposed to the faith in each others' abilities. Truthfully we found our faith in each other as the thing that makes us effective to this day. I know I could pick up the phone and in a heartbeat they would be there.

Recently one of our family members was diagnosed with cancer, and the family/team kicked into action. Phone calls were made, prayers were prayed, and people travelled to be there at the side of those in need. Where did this plan come from? Faith! A standard instilled by my parents: you help him when he needs help, you help her and so on.

They got it right (we didn't always growing up), and that is what makes this model a great team as opposed to a good team. Today I have a saying, "A good team has faith in their talent. A great team has faith in each other." Does this mean we are great? No, it means that the process is. I believe that when I can't, you can! This does work and works every time.

It is what Jesus did for us, when He did what we couldn't. He became man so that He could save us from ourselves. You see, the stuff I found boring and uninteresting was serving a greater purpose than my entertainment, something much bigger than that - life, and not only life, but eternal life. I am so grateful that my mom and dad never took the easy way but took the faith way. Today we can draw upon our own faith in God.

I understand that some of you didn't have the *Leave It to Beaver* home. Broken homes are just as commonplace as ones that aren't. I wish it wasn't that way, but it is. The principle is still the same; faith is out there, it just may not look the same for everyone. However, it is up to us to embrace faith in family, your own family, or some other form of it. Don't give up; God didn't.

My mother had this poster that hung in our basement. All my childhood years through high school, I would walk by this poster. It was even partly torn and worn, much like the words and picture on it. I recently talked to her, and she says it still hangs there. It is a simple picture of a football player, head hanging down, rain and sweat falling off his helmet and face. The inscription says, "Don't Quit" and then below in the corner is a drawing of a black shadow outline of a rocky hillside and a cross with the inscription, "I Didn't."

College

Sports also defined my collegiate career. I was fortunate enough to go to the University of North Dakota to play college baseball. The interesting thing about college was the way it started. Grades were a problem. Looking back it is funny but it wasn't funny at the time. My grade point average at the end of my first semester was 1.2 on a 4-point scale. I was ineligible to continue to play, if my grades didn't come up. In a later chapter, I will talk about this more. I had successfully screwed up in a few short months the whole purpose for being there. I excelled at baseball just not school. Attending a few more classes would have been beneficial.

I quickly realized that change was necessary. I began the process of adding student to my definition. It was hard work. When I finished my decorated baseball career I am proud to say I was known for my physical ability and my  academic ability. Some of the baseball records I posted while at UND are still standing twenty years later. It was a great run and I met some great people, but a professional baseball career as I had dreamed at thirteen years old was not going to happen. I did the next thing a smart collegiate would do I got married. Let the fun begin!

Trudy and I have been married for twenty-one years and have a beautiful daughter Madelyn Grace.

So sports and physicality defined me and would for the next thirty years. What would save me wasn't my physical ability but something far more important: Family, Faith and God.

Chapter 2 – Crazy Story But True

Have you ever sat there waiting for something? I mean something significant. You're waiting in anxious anticipation for it to come. I was sitting with the phone next to me waiting for it to ring. Come on please just ring. I wanted to hear it ring so I could get those butterflies out my stomach and move on. What I would say ran through my mind. *I don't know what I'm doing, what am I going to say?* I'm in over my head! Then it rang. I let it ring again, and nervously I picked it up. I cracked out a sheepish quiet unconfident, "Hello." The voice on the other end was confident, funny but in charge. He simply said, "Hey, Krissy boy! This is

Dennis Morgan in Nashville, Tennessee. You want to make a record?" My life was about to change.

A month earlier I was comfortably serving in my first job out of college, superintendent of parks for my hometown of Williston, North Dakota. It was a great job, especially for a kid just out of school. Trudy, my wife, was comfortably working as well. Life was good. I had the responsibility for taking care of the same ball fields and parks I had once ran and played in as a little boy. It was fun. I was the boss. I wasn't stuck behind a desk. I worked with great people, and I thought life couldn't get any better.

Every year the city of Williston would host a local boat and RV show at the Community Center, a massive ice rink turn convention center in the summer. Boats and RVs are popular in Williston because of its proximity to the banks of the Missouri River. Winters are long and hard, so summer would bring renewal and yearning for the outdoors again. The Boat and RV Show was a big event in this little town. I was in charge of the building, so I was around a lot during the event.

One year the organizers needed to fill a spot

on their free stage with some entertainment, so one of them asked me if I would sing a few songs. I said, "Me? Why me?" They said, "Because you sing. Come on, it will be great."

Now my singing career up until that point was very limited to say the least. Maybe I did the occasional wedding for a friend or a song in church once in a while. A stage? *People, I think you have the wrong guy.*

I would sit in my basement in those days and sing to an audience of two - my dogs Ty and Kiko. I couldn't even get my wife to listen. It wasn't that I didn't like singing; it was just that I enjoyed the basement and my standard crowd, the two dogs. They loved it every time I would sing Garth Brooks, and my beloved little Kiko, a pug/poodle mix, would howl. I would hit a high note, and he would really kick in" "Ooooooo." I preferred that. They were easy to sing in front of; a crowd was a whole different deal.

Then the organizers sweetened the deal. They said, "We will pay you $200." I said, "What time do you want me there?" I knew four songs! I prepped for the big show, my first time to let them hear my four-song tour. *Look out world here I come, move over Garth, Clint, and George. Kris Kuester has just been hired to play the Williston Boat and RV Show Free Stage. Thank you very much, and my four-song show is going to rock!* I thought to myself, *I need a new shirt, some Wranglers, boots, and belt. I need it all, and oh yeah, I need a cowboy hat because all country singers need a good hat.*

The free stage offer made me think back to my first solo. I was probably ten. It was church, and the song was "Zacchaeus." That's right, the one and only. You know it, "Zacchaeus." Come on, sing along:

Zacchaeus was a wee little man,
and a wee little man was he.
He climbed up in a sycamore tree,
For the Lord he wanted to see.
And as the Savior passed him by,
He looked up in the tree,
And He said, "Zacchaeus,
You come down from there;
For I'm going to your house today,
For I'm going to your house today."
Zacchaeus came down from that tree,
As happy as he could be,

> He gave his money to the poor, and said:
> "What a better man I'll be.'"
>
> > - Author Unknown

The play was so good we took it on the road thirty miles to the next town. The tour lasted one show. I thought it had a chance for big things - guess not. But for a ten year old, you have to dream!

Back to the other big show the B&RV tour. I was so nervous I couldn't spit if I wanted. A few people started to gather in the bleachers. The stage was not only free, but also small with a cheesy blue curtain that hung behind it, and that was it the big time! It was then that I realized that four songs at about three minutes per song wouldn't fill thirty minutes; it was more like twelve minutes. What was I going to do for the rest of the show, tell jokes? Panic fell over me. Not only was I going to be bad, but I was going to be bad twice. It was way too late to do anything about it.

There I stood. Then I heard, "Ladies and gentleman, please welcome Williston's very own Kris Kuester." For a moment it was kind of neat to hear my name, but then I realized that ninety-

five percent of the few who had gathered knew me anyway, so what was the point of the introduction? I could have just walked out and greeted everyone by name. "Hey, Bill. Nice to see the Smiths have made it out. And of course, hi, Mom, is Dad coming?" Anyway, I walked out and nervously started my first song; let's just say it was less than impressive. I could hardly breathe. How could these people do this and breathe? I quickly realized that Garth, Clint, and George were probably safe.

I finished my second go round of the same songs I had done just minutes before and finished my music career to a smattering of applause from the locals. I walked off quickly and was met by Trudy. She smiled like always, gave me a big hug, and said, "You were great!" It felt good. I thought for a second what if, and then quickly came back to the moment, to a voice I didn't recognize. He said these words. "Kris Kuester, my name is Charles Walhof and I represent Dennis Morgan in Nashville, Tennessee." *What? Did he say Nashville? SHUT UP!* "You have to be joking. We are in Williston, North Dakota. What are you doing here?" He was tall, maybe mid-forties, his hair was perfectly placed, sunglasses pushed up on the front of his head. He reminded me of Porter Wagoner. He responded to my question, telling me that he had been out west, was heading back towards Nashville, and liked boats and RVs. So he stopped, heard the music, and came over. He continued to speak, because I couldn't. "I liked your songs, especially the second time around." He smiled. See, I knew that was a good plan doing them twice.

The next words out of his mouth would go on to change my life forever! Mr. Walhof said, "How would you to like to record in Nashville?" *Shut your mouth!* "We are in Williston, North Dakota. Nothing happens here except things that are about the town." But he continued, "You have a gift. You need to use it. I think I can help." This doesn't happen in a small town. You go to Nashville, Nashville doesn't come to you. Besides even if you go to Nashville, it doesn't work like that either. You work for years, not thirty minutes.

Okay, where are the cameras? Charles, you are good. Trudy, you are funny. Mom, you were great. You guys had me going for a while. But nope, that wasn't it. It was real. Charles Walhof and I exchanged info, and he said Dennis Morgan would call.

The voice on the other end of line continued to talk, "Krissy, we need to get you down here to Nashville and get working on this record! Are you ready?" I paused for moment, swallowed, and said, "Ah, yeah. Yeah, I guess as ready as I will ever be. Let's do it."

I spent the next six years working in country music. I recorded four records with Dennis Morgan and Charles Walhof. I travelled all over the country and worked with many of the greats at the time Trisha Yearwood, Sawyer Brown, Pam Tillis, Marty Stuart, Chris LeDoux, Jerry Reed, and The Desert Rose Band to name a few.

I told you this story was crazy, but true. You

have to admit that is nuts! A couple of things I have taken away from this are you never know who is watching or listening. Be your best even if you only have four songs in your pocket. You never know where it will get you. It got me a twenty-plus-year career in music, which is still going today. None of this would have ever happened if I had said "no", to the Boat and RV Show.

Chapter 3 - Running Hard

The sound was distinct. I couldn't quite place it. It was like a crunchy, crinkling sound, kind of like paper when you crumple it up. The sun beat down like a heat lamp two inches from my face. Humid was an understatement. What in world was I doing out here? Where was I anyway? The only thing I knew was I wasn't moving! I looked around again to try to figure out the unusual sound. To my left was just highway and the same to my right. Behind me was a field and in front of the same. I listened. It was quiet except for a slight breeze and this strange sound of crumpling paper. Once again my attention turn towards the real problem. Where was I, and how was I going to get out of here?

Ready, Set, Go

My country music career had begun. I had left my job as superintendent of parks to be a Nashville "up and comer." That was different and scary. Just a few days earlier, I was at a party where everyone wished me the best and good luck with the country music. The plane ride was smooth; I hadn't flown much but that was going to change. In fact, travel was going to be the thing I did the most.

People who travel for a living know what I am talking about. You see, when you travel for your job it seems you travel more than anything else, even your job. It is a life that is tough and even grueling at times, in a different way than digging a hole with a shovel or something manual. It drains you emotionally and physically. You begin to use the catch phrase, "Where are we?" as you wake up from some sleep. Here is the myth: "Wow, it must be cool to travel so much and see all you get to see." Sure, for about three months. Then it begins to drain everything you have out of you. Don't get me wrong, I'm not complaining. But the human body and mind was not designed to travel as much as you do when you make Nashville country music "up and comer" your career.

The plane landed smoothly, and it was a relief to be on the ground. I made my way to baggage, and there was my new best friend Charlie - that's right the same one from the Boat and RV show in North Dakota. He came up and asked, "You ready for this?" I said with some hesitation in my voice, "Ahhh, yeah, I guess." "All right," he said,

"Let's go make a record!" It was really happening "Nashville"; I was just in Williston, North Dakota, a few hours before. What happened next was not what I thought it would be; it was not, "Next stop, Grand Ole Opry."

Dreamstreet

Dennis Morgan was taller than I expected. You know how you try to size up people from just a phone conversation, and then when meet them you are never right. Back then it wasn't like today where you can grab your laptop and know everything about somebody you just met. I miss that. The mystery of "What do you look like?" "How tall are you?" or "How do you dress?"

It seemed everybody else I met over the next six years, the more famous they were, the shorter they were. Not Dennis or Charlie, they both were tall. Dennis dressed the same every day I saw him. He didn't look like the big time music mogul I had envisioned, as if I knew what that was. Sport coat, T-shirt, jeans, and his infamous Chuck Taylor tennis shoes. "Mr. Chuck Taylor tennis shoes" was responsible for over three hundred million records sold and hundreds of gold, platinum and multi-platinum albums. His resume is way too long to get into in this book; just Google "Dennis Morgan" and enjoy the ride.

The point was once again what was I doing there? I sang four songs on a free stage in Williston. Come on! I was waiting for the camera crew to come out of the trees and say, "We got you didn't we?" They never showed up, thank you God!

I remember the first time I walked into Dreamstreet, one of the studios Dennis owned for his hit factory. The walls were filled with records platinum, gold, you name it. It seemed every time I looked at a different one, I would say, "You wrote this?" He would just give me a sheepish grin and say, "We sure did, Krissy boy. We sure did."

It was time to start the first record I had ever made, and it was the first time I had been in a studio, let alone a Nashville studio. Did you know that whether you like it or not, more country music is sold than any other genre every year? I guess the country boys got something figured out.

The guys rolled in to start the recording session: Jimmy Hyde (drummer for Eddie Rabitt), Rick Boyer (bassist for Barbara Mandrell), Tim Atwood (keyboards and piano for the Grand Old Opry Staff Band), Jim Horn (plays anything you blow air into and with everybody), and Morgan handled anything guitar. I thought, *You have to be joking.* From four songs to this. It was a bit surreal,

to say it lightly. That's the way it started. It was hard work, long sessions, fast food, and funny stories. We finished the album then hit the road and for the next six years, I repeated that process four times. Make a record, then hit the road to promote, play, and sell product. For a while you are all jacked up on the high, the newness, and the way they treat you. The road and the music business are brutal - miles and miles on the road playing anything and everywhere. That is the definition of an "up and comer." You pay your dues. Yes, we had tours that were very cool, nice stuff, accommodations, and food. However, as a new recording artist, that certainly isn't the norm.

Need a Band

The first thing was to get a band. Remember, I was a "4 song man" with just a guitar and no band. Let me introduce you to three guys that I respect greatly to this day. They were there in the beginning right to the painful end. Dean Vestal, a guitarist who had so much talent he could have made a living just playing sessions and never travelling. Taggart Snyder, a keyboard specialist and master of all electronic things that make sound. Tom Ator, my brother in law who did everything and anything we needed. These three guys played every show with me from show one, every crappy bar, casino, convention, and even the stages were you couldn't see the end of the people. The rest were hired guns, but Dean, Tag, and Tom were like family.

REC and the Flash Pods

We started small. Charlie booked us

anywhere he could get us: bars, fairs (free stages - hey, that sounded familiar), or the local county REC convention. If you could think it, we would do it, and not for much money because we knew it would pay off later. I remember one Regional Electric Co-Op event we were doing, I think in Iowa somewhere. We had just bought some new lights called "flash pods." The idea was you hit the flashes at the end of a song or during a special part, and we would become silhouettes - pretty cool. A flash pod is actually an aircraft landing light; they are very bright to say the least. You can't even look directly at them or they will temporarily blind you. So you make sure they are set right, since they are behind you. That night in sound check we took extra time to make sure everything was right, because "do this show right and it would lead to more work."

These gigs, although a bit boring, paid well, and there were a lot of them to go around. Now these shows usually went like this: 1,000 farmers would pack into a gym somewhere for their annual meeting, eat, do some voting for new officers, and then bring on the entertainment. Did I say the audience is mostly elderly? Just don't get too crazy, no fireworks, explosions, or pyro stuff. (Like the Chris LeDoux tour, who hired the former KISS pyro guy and constantly blew things up. When we worked with him, his manager would stand on the side of the stage and roll his hand around in a circle, "one more." Until it got dark.) No, these were simple people expecting Pat Boone to walk on but somehow we got these gigs. This is what an "up and comer" did, but at the same time we were constantly trying to spice it up a bit push the envelope a little.

Showtime! The pudding had been served, officers selected, "Ladies and gentlemen, please welcome Nashville Recording Artist, Kris

Kuester." A kind welcome of applause, and bam a song. We opened every show with "Tennessee Homecoming," a song Dennis Morgan and Paul Overstreet had written, an up-tempo country roller. It was perfect, fun, fast, and we played the snot out of it.

Everything was rolling along perfectly; the crowd was clapping and having fun. Little did the first fifteen rows know, but something was coming their way that they were not expecting. Can someone say, "Pass out the radiation goggles?" You got it, we arrived at the big finish. The new lights were to come on, and come on they did, right into the first fifteen rows! They blinded everyone as they tried to shield their eyes. I stood in horror trying to sing the final note and also trying to get the tech's attention in the back of the room, to kill the lights. They thought this was cool - the effect had worked. Wrong! It had blinded innocent farmers and their wives fifteen rows deep. Nice move, "up and comer." Lesson learned: maybe less is more. You sing and play just fine, save the special effects for the pros.

Pay Off

For the next six years we worked our tail off. We played everywhere, slowly but steadily climbing the ladder. Each record brought more gigs, each gig brought more success, and more success brought us closer to our goal - sign the big record deal. As I said before, we did tours with Trisha Yearwood, Sawyer Brown, Pam Tillis, Chris

LeDoux, Marty Stuart, Jerry Reed, and The Desert Rose Band, to mention a few. We were so close.

Which brings me back to that strange noise I was hearing at the beginning of this chapter. We had broken down in the middle of nowhere, Nebraska. We needed to get to Northern Minnesota for a big show. The sound? Well, that was the corn growing. Yes, you can actually hear it. It is not a myth, it's true, and it sounds like crumpling paper. Finally, we got rescued from our demise and made it to the show, but for a while it seemed we would have to cancel. I am proud to say that in our six year run, we never missed a single show!

Chapter 4 - Golf Course and a Doctor

Isn't it ironic that in life you hold a particular opinion of something only to completely retract it later? That pretty much sums up my relationship with the game of golf. There was a day that I thought nothing of the game and never played. It seemed to me to be the game of the privileged. The country clubs and social events were not exactly my scene. My sports were more of the traditional type - baseball, football, and basketball. They all involved some kind of running, catching,

and throwing. Golf was stand there and hit a stationary ball and try to get it in the hole. Now don't get me wrong. I never said it was easy, but it just seemed pointless. Why was I standing on a tee box in Montana with total strangers? One answer: my wife made me do it.

Let's Tee One Up

I had spent the last six years of my life chasing a dream of being a big-time country music star. To be honest, I was close. I mean really close to breaking through to the next level. From four songs to four records later, established in the Nashville music scene, working with Grammy Award winning Dennis Morgan and our road guide Charlie Walhof. Why? We had been given a chance, and we jumped in without regret. It was paying off, but after six years I was tired. So Trudy and I took a much-needed vacation.

The morning was nice. It was moving towards fall, but still some golf was left to play before the winter set in. In my group of strangers was a doctor. I don't remember his name just his occupation. At thirty, I was still in great shape. Even with all the games played, I could still hold my own in a pickup game of anything. However, this was golf. I could only hit it a long way. That was my strategy. Let's just say that's not how you score well in golf.

Today, it is everything I love about the game - show to get the ball to places when you can't do things you used to be able to. Watching me play a round of golf now is downright hilarious. We often joke about the fact that everybody that sees me from a fairway away must think I have spent most of the day on the nineteenth hole as opposed to the course, but more on that later. Now back to the match at hand.

We had made it through six holes without losing too many balls or me losing my mind out of frustration. I was just out there for fun. On the seventh hole, the doctor asked, "Kris you don't mind if I ask you a question do you?" I replied, "No, of course not." So he said, "What happen to your leg?"

I had noticed a slight limp in my right leg; I didn't think much of it. I had always walked funny, very pigeon-toed, and a funny gate, but nothing that had slowed me down. I said, "You know I don't know. I think it is my hip, from all the sports. I think I'm just wearing out." He responded, "I don't want to diagnose you here on a golf course, but I don't think it is your hip. You see you have a slight vibration in your gate, when you walk you have some spasticity. That is usually something neurological. You should get it checked out."

Wow! Neurological? What the heck does that mean? I wasn't sure what to say. I think he half expected me to know what was wrong, bringing to reason why he asked the question in the first place. I didn't and I hadn't; it never had even crossed my mind. Spasticity? I was in great shape, maybe a little sore at times but athletically I could still hold my own. I replied hesitantly, "Sure, I'll umm, do that." *Spasticity, get out of here! Me, the once great athlete, decorated for his accomplishments, and fit as could be.* There was nothing wrong with me, I thought as, I ripped another bomb of a drive. *There is your spasticity!*

We finished the rest of the round without too much conversation. However, my mind was not on the game but on what this doctor had said. "You should get that checked out." I thanked them for the round and promised I would follow up on the leg thing. I headed back to where we were staying to find Trudy.

At dinner, I told her about the doctor and what he had said. She said with a sense of urgency in her voice, "Yes, right away, we need to do that Kris." We left the next day back to Williston. My mind couldn't leave the thoughts of the golf and the doctor. I began to wonder, What if he's right? What could it be? Who would we go see? What was this thing?

I still had some time when we got back before returning to road. We were close to hitting it big in music. Little did I know, that time was about to change significantly.

Trudy worked in the health industry and had connections that referred us to the best in the area. She set up an appointment with the one recommended, a neurologist in Billings, Montana, about 300 miles away. We prepared for the trip.

Ironic

Golf today is my refuge; the game I once hated has become the one thing I can do fairly well. I will play anywhere, anytime, and on any course. We were visiting my brother Kurt and his family for Thanksgiving a couple of years ago in Chicago. Chicago isn't exactly warm on Thanksgiving, but I said to my brother, "Hey lets go golfing!" He looked at me and said, "It is twenty-nine degrees outside!" I said "Yeah, but it isn't snowing."

So being the good sport he is, we grabbed every possible warm coat, sweater, gloves, and hat we could find and headed out for the course. It was closed, duh. But he said, "Well, we can just take one bag and hoof it. You up for it?" I smiled and said, "Bring it on." It was one of the most enjoyable things I have ever done in my life. Nine holes of

walking and hitting a ball across ice and snow was just beautiful. We stopped on the seventh hole, sat on a bench, and talked about life and how blessed we were. To this day the seventh is a special hole to me on any course, anywhere, anytime. Ironic, don't you think?

Chapter 5 - The Diagnosis

The worst part of a diagnosis is the waiting. If you talk to anyone with major illness, they will say not knowing is worse than the diagnosis. Once you have been diagnosed, then you can begin the process of healing, not just physically but spiritually and emotionally. It is almost a relief.

Neuro

The office of the neurologist had a clean solid door, with the various different doctors listed.

Trudy and I entered slowly, not knowing what was on the other side. We found a fairly quiet waiting room. It struck me for some reason that I had played almost twenty-five years of some kind of sport and had never been injured. I never needed to go to a doctor other than routine physicals let alone a specialist.

I then looked up, saw several nurses gathered at the reception desk, and for some reason before we spoke a word their eyes spoke many. The look they had was odd, as if they had seen this before, and it wasn't a good thing. We filled out the necessary miles of paperwork and then returned to the desk. "Please have seat, Mr. Kuester, and the doctor will see you in a minute." I always laugh at that, "The doctor will see you in a minute." *How do they count minutes in the medical profession? By way of the sundial, a minute turns into a half hour. I'm sure you have experienced this before, the endless wait to see the doctor.*

Finally a nurse came out and said, "Mr. Kuester?" We stood up and started to move towards the door. Our lives would never be the same; the diagnosis had begun. We slipped through the door following the nurse, through a maze of hallways to another room, and, you guessed it, another wait. "Please wait here and the doctor will be in." I almost wanted to finish her statement but didn't. I was feeling a bit anxious and scared.

In walked a doctor. I don't even remember his name - it didn't matter. We wouldn't be with him for very long, just long enough to find out something was very wrong.

The first test he did on me was a hot and cold sensation test, basically to see if I could feel temperature on the body. It seemed odd, but not as odd as the results. Over the next several minutes they quickly noticed that a majority of the right side of my body had no hot and cold sensation. "What? You must be joking. Test it again," I nervously demanded. This couldn't be, I would have known. They did the test again, and I could not distinguish hot or cold water with my right hand and a majority of the right side of my body. I didn't even know it! Then came the next test, a pinprick to see if the surface sensory was gone also. Sure enough, it was. Nothing. They were sticking pins in my arm, and I couldn't feel anything.

What was going on? I felt fine, I was strong. It is what defined me, my physicality. Now, I was being told that I couldn't feel hot and cold or whether a pin was being stuck in my body. I was in trouble; the looks I saw when I entered were dead on. They knew they had seen this before. Others who had walked in not knowing and then leaving changed people forever.

They quickly elevated me to neurosurgery. They said, "We have done all we can do, and you will have to undergo further tests to figure out what is going on." My body was masked with outer strength while being short-circuited from the inside out.

Dr. Wood and the MRIs

My neurosurgeon was Dr. Wood. This name I wouldn't forget because of the amount of time we were going to spend together. He was a no nonsense guy without much of a personality. Later we would have some laughs together, but not now. He immediately ordered three days of testing to aggressively go after the cause of the problem. It was brutal; I was put in and tested by every device the medical world had to offer.

One session I remember very distinctly was a three-hour journey in the tube of an old style MRI machine. I had never experienced one. In fact, I had never been in the hospital before. I was getting ready to stay awhile. The old MRI machine was not designed for someone with broad Scandinavian shoulders. As I went in, my shoulders bent a little to fit in the tube. Not a good feeling. The top of the tube seemed like I could lick it with my tongue. Anxiety began to rack my body. "Let me out of here!" my brain screamed. I was ready to squeeze the button as I tossed up prayers to the God I trusted, and fortunately He was listening. I calmed down, and three hours later, out I came. I was stiff, could barely walk. Then it was on to the next device. This was the process repeated for three days.

Finally on day three of test central, we were brought back to Dr. Wood's office. They had found it, the cause for the spasticity and nerve damage. Although I was scared, it was almost over, no more tests, please no more waiting, just tell us. Trudy gripped my hand and squeezed it hard in anticipation. Then Wood just said it with no emotion. "We have found nine tumors in your spinal cord." "Cancer?" Trudy began to cry; I showed no emotion. My tears would come later. "No, not cancer," he said "It's syringomyelia." "What? What is syringomyelia?" I couldn't even pronounce it, let alone having ever heard of it. He began to describe what little they knew about SM. I heard little, but I did hear this: that it was incurable and that it was neurodegenerative.

What once had defined me was now leaving me and fast. I had nine syrinxes starting at Cervical 6 and going all the way down to Thoracic 12. They needed to do something now, or I was going to be a quadriplegic or even worse, dead.

Dr. Wood said, "I'm sorry"; no emotion just words. I almost felt sorry for him, I'm sure he had done this hundreds of times before, delivered the bad news to a family. He said, "Let's get together tomorrow, and we will go over your options."

Dinner that night was not real tasty. We didn't talk much, we were just in shock. *Oh my goodness! What are we going to do? This was too much.* Incurable and neurodegenerative, translation *we can't do much if anything, and no matter what we do you are going to get worse. That is a life forecast nobody wants to hear, but it was ours.*

We returned to the hotel after picking through our dinner. When we got back, something happened that I would never forget. Every time I speak somewhere telling our story, I never leave this next part out. We knelt beside our bed and cried out to this God we professed to believe in, and just said, "This is too big for us, you have to take this God." These words of Jesus rang in my head:

> *"Come to me, all you who are weary and*
> *burdened, and I will give you rest. Take*
> *my yoke upon you and learn from me,*
> *for I am gentle and humble in heart,*
> *and you will find rest for your souls.*
> *For my yoke is easy and my*
> *burden is light."*
> ### Matthew 11:28–30 NIV

We finished our simple prayer. We didn't ask for healing but simply for Him to take this burden. He would.

Options

The next morning we were up early. There

was still not too much conversation as we headed back to the hospital for the treatment options. Dr. Wood met us at his office, his demeanor the same almost monotone, without emotion just information. "Kris, we have two options right now with SM. In your case, we can try a spinal cord surgery where we enter the cord and try to drain the tumors. However, it is risky, and the results have been mixed. The other option is an experimental procedure, where we place a peritoneal shunt in your brain close to the stem. We think there is a possible tear in your cord at the brain stem. We would enter your brain and insert a shunt with a tube. A pump on the side of your head will drain the excess spinal fluid away from your cord then route it into your abdomen, where your body would just absorb and re-use it." I asked him, "Has anyone ever gotten better with either treatment?" He said "No, but the shunt procedure has shown some good results in keeping the progression of

SM at bay for longer."

Nice choices. Today, I joke about the third unknown option - the dream where we go home and everybody is all right. Back then it was pretty bleak. We chose the brain surgery. It just sounded like it had a better chance at keeping my quality of life longer. Both procedures had terrible track records and a lot of risk. We began the process of preparing for the surgery. The doctor said, "We need to go now." The surgery was scheduled for one week later. It was like buying a car; okay, we will take the blue one! Unfortunately, it was my brain and my spinal cord and not a car.

One week came fast - just enough time for us to get home, pack some stuff and turn around and head back to Montana. Calls from my family began to pour in. Remember, there were no cell phones, but I remember the first to call was my

brother Todd. He was my roommate and my best friend all through our childhood. We were one grade apart in school so we bunked together. We had been through so much together. We had played sports together especially baseball. Although we didn't play college ball together, we turned plenty of double plays growing up. If we got a chance to turn one over, nine times out of ten we did. He was a great athlete. We had walked through some rough times some years earlier, and now he was coming to my side. We cried. I remember he kept saying he was so sorry, over and over. I am sure he would have taken my place if he could have, and I would do the same for him, even today. The whole family called over the course of the next few days before we left for Deaconess Medical Center. I felt very loved, but I would be lying if I said I wasn't scared.

Brain Surgery

The surgery was scheduled to last about six hours. The last thing I remember was counting back from one hundred. I think I hit ninety-eight. The next thing I heard was this faint cry for help, "Help me, please someone help me." It was faint, and it was an elderly voice. I opened my eyes and turned towards the voice. It was a woman in post-op with me, and she was crying out for help. The next thing was my head. I wasn't even sure it was still attached to my body it hurt so much. A nurse was soon at my side. "Mr. Kuester, are you doing okay?" I tried to move my arms to touch my head, but I couldn't move them or my legs. Next I thing I remember, I was moving towards my room. That room became my nemesis. I would do anything to get out of there from that moment on, if only it was a moment.

The next few days were a blur, with blistering headaches and rehab that was awful, to put it lightly. As long as Trudy was there I felt like I was okay. The first night was awful. My parents had made the trip with us, and they were a great support. That night they all went back to the hotel, and I was there with a morphine drip and the nursing staff. Did I say brutal? Well, let me say it again.

The next night, Trudy being the person she is, said, "I'm not going anywhere." She forced the

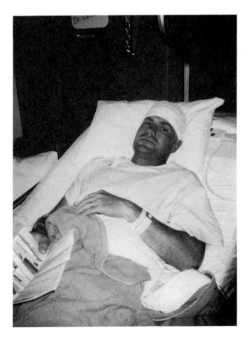

nurses to bring in another bed so she could stay with me. I didn't want to be alone. I didn't miss the mark when I asked her to marry me. "For better or worse" - well, welcome to worse. And there she was, rolling in beds to stay at my side. The shunt was making me incredibly sick, and it was almost unbearable. It is like the worst fair ride you have ever been on, and then just add a whole bunch more spins. Some days I just wanted them to take it back out, and I would take my chances. One day it got so bad, Trudy helped them decide to go back in and see what was wrong. Here came brain surgery number two. The pump they had

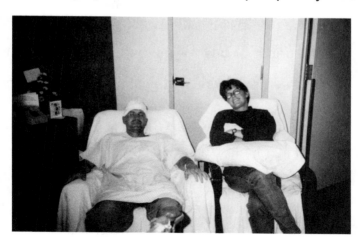

installed was moving too much fluid, and it was the cause for the unbearable nausea and dizziness. The recovery after the second surgery was better but by no means a walk in the park. The days to come would just get worse. I might have quit if I had known just how hard the next year would be. It would almost kill me.

After months in the hospital I was released to go back to Williston and continue my rehab, although after my surgery I had lost my ability to walk and had limited use of my arms. Dr. Wood assured me it would slowly come back, only then to slowly go away again. Hopefully, the shunt would keep it at bay for as long as possible, and the nine syrnexes would stay at nine. That was the prayer and hope!

I started this chapter with the statement about the wait is worse than the knowing. Well, it is true. Sometimes it takes time and now was my time to redefine. It just took longer and was harder than I thought it would be. Today I wouldn't have changed it for anything, or you wouldn't be reading this. It wouldn't be helping you cope with your "it."

Chapter 6 - The Year Of Hell

Sometimes I hear from people, "Why do think God let this happen?" The answer is, "I don't know, I'm not even sure He had anything to do with it. Rather it is a product of a fallen world." "Good" people don't even exist according to author Phillip Yancey. He could be right. Read Romans 3:10-18 and you get a picture of his theory.

I believe that "sin" is the problem. All of us are born into it, and good deeds don't qualify you as "good" or "righteous." Only Jesus' death on a cross qualifies you to become righteous in His sight. This is earth and not heaven. Life is not easy. The reward comes later in heaven, because of what Christ did and the acceptance of that gift. This gift is not free - Jesus paid for it - but the receiving it is free. It goes way beyond the problems we face while here on earth, so spend your time on the blessing and not on the storm. Not easy to do when you are the one facing the "it."

I was wheeling and not walking as I left Deaconess Hospital. My time there for now was done and it felt good. My body didn't though. The shunt continued to be a challenge for me, and it got worse. It had been two months since the first surgery. I had lost a ton of weight. I was a shell of the athletic thirty-year-old "up and comer" music star. I was shuffling around now for short periods of time. A big advance in my time there; I walked in and now I was fighting to get better. I was tired and depression was about to take hold of me in a way I had never dreamed it could.

A Car Ride and What?

We had made it about a hundred miles toward home when we decided to stop for a moment. The movements of the car only made me feel awful. I couldn't get my bearings. I was constantly dizzy and nausea. It is even hard to write about it today, some fifteen years later because it takes me back to a time that I just as soon forget. I was getting ready to have my first panic attack, and it gave no warning. I was standing by the car just getting some fresh air, when all of the sudden this rush of adrenaline seem to fill my body. I thought I was having a heart attack, and I thought I was dying. I cried out for Trudy. I began to try to move away, shuffling, wandering. Where I was going I don't know, but I just had to move. I would have run, but I couldn't. Trudy ran over to me asking what was wrong. I said in a panic-stricken voice trembling, "I can't breathe, I think I am dying!" Her look was horror, which just made me feel worse. She had never experienced this either; she tried her best to calm me down. "Just breathe. Relax. You're fine. You're going be just fine." My head was swirling. I could barely stand up. Trudy slowly moved me over to the car where the door was open and helped sit me back down. "Here drink some water," she gently offered. I sipped the water still confused and wondering, *What was that?* Sweating profusely, I then began to regain my bearings. Trudy continued to say, "You're going to be all right. Just relax. Easy, I'm here. I'm not going anywhere." Her words were comforting.

After what seemed forever, it was over. It actually had only been a couple of minutes, but they were two minutes of terror. *What happened?* I thought. As we returned to our journey home, I wanted to go back to the hospital. The place I had grown to detest was now where I wanted to be. It was a safe place, but I hated everything about it at the same time. I had just experienced my first "panic attack." It wouldn't be the last.

Somehow, we made it through the 300-mile journey mostly because of Trudy. If the dictionary had pictures, she would appear in a lot of places; the word "tough" would be one of them. Little did we know she was about to take control of holding a world of confusion, panic attacks, dark depression, and a sick husband, all at one time. How she did it still baffles me today. Where did her strength come from? I thought I was tough - compared to her, I was wimp!

The days rolled into weeks. I couldn't work.

I could barely go outside without feeling the side effects of the shunt; I just couldn't get my bearings. It was confusing; I was dizzy all of the time and spent most of my days at home alone sitting. *Why? What had happened?* I was healthy just a few months earlier, standing on a golf course with three other guys thinking about the next move in my career. Now I was unable to work and not even able to walk more than a few feet without help.

Trudy worked for a physical therapist, so my therapy sessions were done under her watchful eye and tender love, but with tough words of encouragement. "Come on, Kris, just one more. You can do it. You are getting better." I wanted to quit so many times and would have; then today you wouldn't be reading these pages. I would be crumpled up in some corner full of self-pity. Here is what I learned the hard way about self-pity: the more I did it the more it created. Self-pity just creates more self-pity. Thank God, Trudy wouldn't stand for it, ever! Some days she flat out wouldn't have it. "Get up. We are going." As much as I would plead "no," she would drive harder. Trudy taught me, "Never quit, ever!"

Depression

Even with the love and support of Trudy and my family, I began to slide into a deep depression. I couldn't stop it. In my mind I was now worthless. What was I going to do? I didn't see any light at the end of any tunnel. My purpose was gone;

what defined me before was no longer there and never would be again. Who was I anyway? I couldn't even work, let alone walk for more than a few steps. My arms had come back pretty good, however my right one had developed searing pain from time to time. Syringo was moving quickly, and parts of it were not going to be stopped even by the best medicine had to offer. That's the part called incurable. *Even now as I type this part of the book, my right arm is on "fire." I have to stop for moments to allow Syringo to do its thing, just wait for it to pass. I suck at typing anyway, so it is a good excuse to take a break.*

I know this may sound like a broken record, but without the love, support, and drive of my wife, Trudy, I would have packed it up a long time ago. I was unable to work, we still had bills, and we were not sitting on a pot of gold. She worked three jobs just so we could squeak by. That is another part I never leave out when I speak to audiences. Two things got me through this year of hell - God and His angel Trudy. It wasn't my strength and still isn't today. Someday, Trudy will get to heaven and they will just say, "That was very impressive." This makes me emotional, just thinking about it. All of this was a part of the process in redefining me.

The darkest time of the year of hell was when I finally had to visit a psychologist. I had gotten so bad that I wouldn't even listen to reason. My mother took me to these sessions. Trudy was working and couldn't go everywhere, every time. My parents would help anytime we needed them. They were great but going to a psychologist office wasn't. Don't get me wrong they are needed, and people definitely benefit from their expertise. I just couldn't figure out how I had fallen so low so fast.

Walking in the office of the psychologist

was just brutal. We lived in a town of 12,000 people, everybody knew everybody in some way, and everybody definitely knew me or at least my name. Sure enough, the receptionist who I don't remember today knew me. "Hey Kris, nice to see you." "Yeah, you too." I was thirty years old, with my mother in the psych office. Come on, you got to see the humor in that. It is right out of a comedy. Just picture: Will Ferrell with his mother in a psych office. However, I was Kris Kuester defined as you heard it before. It was flat out sad. My sessions with the doctor were uncomfortable. First of all, I couldn't understand why I was there and couldn't get better on my own. At the same time, I didn't want to feel the way I did anymore, not for another minute. They didn't help, other than give me some drugs that made me feel dizzier than I did before. The psych relationship didn't last long, thank God!

The Mailbox

Each day I continued to battle the demons of SM and its idiotic friends, depression, anxiety, and panic, all the while working harder as my strength came back. The physical therapy sessions were beginning to pay off. Progress for the first time began to show itself. We gladly accepted these small victories with quiet celebrations. One day in the silence of our home, as I sat in my trusty chair where I spent many hours talking to God, even arguing with Him at times, I noticed our mailbox. I decided to make an attempt to get the mail. Pretty exciting day, the mail. "Yeah! I will get the mail." My contribution to the family unit. I thought, *Pathetic*, but also I thought, *Why not?* I wasn't supposed to venture out without help because of my physical condition and fragility of my spinal cord. One fall could snap my cord, and I would be paralyzed. The risk to me at the time was worth it! Wait a minute, you are saying to yourself, you were willing to risk snapping your spinal cord to get the mail?

Yes! That is how low I had gotten, or maybe that's how driven I was to get better. I didn't know how God would use this simple, but huge act for me to change my whole world.

I remember standing at the back door almost like a little kid sneaking out of his house. Would someone see me and tell Trudy? I didn't care. I was going to go for it. I sized it up with military precision like a good general devising some battle plan. It looked like maybe a hundred steps or so. I would later find out exactly how many. Here we go, drum roll please. I made it ten steps and almost threw up and almost fell down twice. I retreated, *mailbox 1: me 0*. This process carried itself out over the next couple of weeks, me versus the mailbox, with me losing every time. I was getting further each time. Ten to twenty, twenty to thirty. The battle was on in this war to recapture my identity and purpose. It all had to do with a mailbox.

I never told Trudy about the mailbox adventure for fear that she would squash the self-prescribed therapy. The battle that had been ensuing between these two foes raged on. I had hit fifty a couple of times and sixty. Then one day I told myself, "We are getting the mail today if we have to crawl!" So out I went, ten, twenty, shuffling along like an eighty-year-old man. A far cry from who I once was. Twenty steps turned to thirty and then forty, fifty, and sixty, and then seventy. I couldn't believe it! I was not going to be denied eighty. "Can you feel it?" Cue the music. Ninety steps, today it is was mine. Mr. Mailbox, you will go down in defeat. One hundred! It was one hundred exactly. I made it. I had gotten the mail. I half expected a marching band to come out of the bushes or something, but it was just the mail, my mailbox and me. That was the point in my life that I found purpose again. It was the first time that I

had done something on my own without help or assistance, just me.

After a moment of internal celebration, I realized I was on an "island" and I had to get back. High on adrenaline and the voice of Trudy in my head ("You can do it, Kris"), I made it back to the house and headed for my chair, all the way clutching the mail. It was mine. I held it like it was a trophy.

I sat in the chair and waited for Trudy to return from working one of her jobs. I never moved from that chair for six and a half hours waiting for her to show her what I had done. Then finally I heard the back door open. I stood up on my wobbly legs and moved towards where she was and greeted her clutching the mail. With tears in my eyes and tears in hers, I said, "I got the mail today," holding it up, and she simply responded through the tears in her eyes, "Good for you, good for you."

There wasn't anything else to say, we had crossed a point we had been praying about for almost a year. It was a feeling that is indescribable, a point when you know you can do it again, whatever that is. We had been praying together and alone for so long, "God, please where are you, please help us," and He finally showed Himself! You see He had been there the whole time in Trudy. He was using her willingness to help and encourage me. Finally, through a little thing like the mail, it sent us over the edge to redefining our lives.

It didn't happen overnight from there, but it started to happen, much faster than before. Now everything became a "mailbox" to me. I was on the hunt to conquer more of them and redefine.

Chapter 7 - Being Redefined

Being redefined for me was a process that began the moment I had reached my infamous goal a "mailbox." It still amazes me how this part of the "Living With It" story continues to move people. I think it is because everybody has an "it" in life, maybe multiple ones all at the same time, and it can become overwhelming. Believe me, I know where you are, but hold on for hope is coming your way, even if you can't see it. You are not alone. Dealing with your particular "it" will require your full

attention and focus; the "it" won't go away. You will face it sometime, if you want to be all you can be and all God wants you to be in life.

For me it began with a job. I needed purpose again. It didn't matter what it was. I was willing to do anything. My friend Brad, now superintendent of parks for Williston, the position I had held prior to signing my record deal, was the first one I asked. He said, "Kris, I don't have anything really. All I have are these picnic tables. Those need to be painted. I would never have you do that. You used to run this place." Without hesitation I said, "Yes. Please, yes I'll take it." I had my first job beginning to be redefined. It paid five bucks an hour, and I was going to be the best picnic table painter on the planet. I was in a small room with a brush and some tables. The paint was red. I still remember that vividly.

Being redefined doesn't mean it is easy, it just means you have a way out towards becoming the person you want to be. Maybe you may have to swallow your pride, accept the gift, and "start painting." That was fifteen years ago. Things have changed, but now back to the paint story.

My painting career didn't last a long time, but I am forever grateful to Brad for the chance to begin to redefine. He may not think about it, but I do every time I pick up a paintbrush. After that my dad mentioned to me one day, "You should go up to the church and ask them if you can help." "Doing what?" I responded. He said, "They do music, maybe you can help with that." Doubt began to fill my mind. Remember panic, anxiety, and depression? They were still hanging around. I thought, *Who would want me?* Especially this version of me: broken, physically and emotionally. I was less than moved to act.

Return to Music

After a while, I began to pickup my guitar again and started to play and sing in my basement. I was almost back to where I was some six years earlier. The crowd had changed a little. My dog Kiko had been replace by Spitzy, a Miniature Schnauzer, with as much talent for the high notes as little Kiko. Ty was still the mainstay; he made every basement show for years. As my musical gift began to return, I gained confidence and skill.

My dad's words began to make sense. I had also studied what these "church guys" were doing. They were called "worship leaders." It was music again, but for a higher purpose. Instead of playing for record sales, it was playing for God. I couldn't think of anything more important than that. Was I the guy for the job, if they had one? Remember I was the guy who intensely argued with God not long before about the condition I was in and why

He wasn't answering all of these prayers that were being lifted up. He was. His plan was different, and much better than mine.

The time had come for the big move. Music again? I couldn't imagine that was what God had in mind, but I was willing to find out. I had studied everything about the job of worship leaders. I did believe that I could do it, but I stilled struggled about it and my new self.

I set the meeting up with the church people. They were both friends of mine, and they were really excited. I unconfidently said, "Do you think I could do this?" They said without hesitation "Yes!" I hadn't expected that, that was easy, but I asked, "How would I get up on the platform?" They responded, "One step at a time."

This was the beginning of new way to move

around physically, a challenge to this day I have to deal with. I call it wall walking. I could never be a good thief, I touch everything in sight as I maneuver around, bouncing off walls and anything that I can find. It is a science; I have become an expert wall walker. When necessary, I pull out my buddy "Hugo", my cane aptly named for its now worn brand name from Wal-Mart for fifteen dollars. We have been a lot of places together.

I was a natural worship leader. Besides the obvious limp, that was a part of the new me. I slid into this new position of church musician. Much like the country music days, I was able to naturally move with the audience, and now with God in my heart able to lead worshippers. I was hooked and purpose had returned. I worked very hard and not for money, because there was not much to have. They hadn't planned on having a new position, but somehow they made it possible for me to start. I quickly began to befriend the other pastors in the city. I loved to do things together when we could. Denominations didn't really mean that much to me, since my days with Athletes In Action in college, where we had come from every background and denominations for a single purpose. I still believe today we make too much of denominations and not enough about God. I feel that I have enjoyed beauty in all of the churches and denominations I have been privileged to worship with over the last fifteen years.

One day I had lunch with a fellow pastor friend, who was the pastor of another church across town. He told me he was leaving to take a new position out of state. I was bummed, but happy for him. My last words to him were, "Don't forget about me" and he didn't, he would later help me land my second worship leader position.

My strength was coming back, and my handle on my three buddies panic, anxiety, and depression was seemingly under control. I was happy my medical reports were good. The shunt was doing what it was supposed to I was feeling good; my redefinition was in full swing!

Merriam Webster defines "redefined" this way:

1: to define (as a concept) again: reformulate
<had to redefine their terms>

2 a: to reexamine or reevaluate especially with a view to change b: transform

Redefining oneself is a very difficult thing to do, but anything is possible if you believe that to be true. I am living proof of that. Over the course of that last fifteen years God has used me in more ways than I could have done in my previous career. Don't get me wrong, I loved country music - it was good. What God has done over the last fifteen

years is great, but all of this came from a diagnosis that was less than encouraging. I wasn't supposed to be walking; God thought differently. I shouldn't have accomplished this much in my industry; God thought differently. When God gets involved things happen! He moves with perfect speed and grace. He muscles His way through if necessary, gently loves when needed, and blesses beyond measure. None of us deserve anything, but He continues to do things. Thinking about that cracks me up and causes me to laugh out loud.

Resume after Syringo

Director of Music

Gloria Dei Lutheran Church

Williston, North Dakota

Worship Pastor

Red Cedar Community Church

Rice Lake, Wisconsin

Executive Pastor of Arts

Cypress Wesleyan Church

Columbus, Ohio

Vice President of Development / Chaplin

Integrity Bank

Atlanta, Georgia

Worship Leader

Goshen Valley Boys Ranch

Waleska, Georgia

Executive Pastor of Arts

Richmond Community Church

Richmond, Virginia

Founder/Executive Director

Living With It Ministries

Atlanta, Georgia

Four New Worship Records Recorded

"Jesus is Lord"	1997
"Healing Love"	1998
"Kris Kuester Live"	2002
"Work in Progress"	2009

Author of "Redefined"   2010

In the last fifteen years, I have accomplished more with God's help than in the previous thirty years. Have people done more than me? Absolutely. That isn't the point. We aren't the few that gain national recognition for their accomplishments.

Today, I am on the endless pursuit for joy for the rest of my life. Most days you will find me laughing, enjoying the ride, and always looking forward to the next thing God will do. I guess God had a purpose for my life when I didn't. He knew that it was there. I just had to take a step, just one. Mine was towards my mailbox.

Chapter 8 – $F^3 \times G = J$

"Your grade point average is 1.2, if you don't get it up you won't be able to baseball anymore." I was horrified! *You can't be serious. I have to play baseball, it is the reason I am here.* The truth is you actually have to pass classes to play the sport you love. Novel concept. This was the conversation I had with my college baseball coach after my first semester at UND. That's bad, almost like the movie, Animal House. "Blutarsky, you have no grade point average!"

School never really moved me, hence the position I found myself in after just one semester. Formulas, math, science were a total bore, yawn. Redefine is not about boring or not boring, it is about what you need to do to overcome your "it" and become all you want to be and all that God wants you to be in life. That redefining experience for me was not difficult. I wasn't dumb or learning disabled, just lazy. The formula that later would redefine me was already in process. I went to class, played baseball, and never dealt with that again.

Defining Your "It"

I talk to people every day all over the country that tell me about their "it," how it is affecting their life or holding them back from their full potential. "Its" at times can be heartbreaking. These are stories of real people who are truly hurting, trying to figure out what or if anything is next for them and their life. At the same time, I meet as many with incredible stories of courage and comeback from things far worse than anything I have encountered. They rose to successes I could only dream about.

Here is what I have learned about the "it" in your life. It is not comparable to anyone else's story of comeback or rise or fall. Your "it" is exclusive to you. That is critical to remember. Never compare your situation to anyone else, for as you deal with the "it" in your life, you will find "its" are relative. You don't need to have a physical deficiency, cancer, addiction, or anything else the world would deem as a major crisis. Nor does your redefinition need to result in you becoming a movie star, CEO, great athlete, or something the world has classified as successful. The "it" and the redefining result are all relative. To what? To you and where you are in life.

My daughter is five years old, and her "it"

is that we don't have pancakes for breakfast. Could be insignificant to you, major to her. Take somebody like my dad. Nobody knows him outside of his small circle. He worked three jobs for most of his life so his children could wear Levis and Nike tennis shoes, and every one of his seven kids graduated from college. Maybe not so significant to you, but ask his children what they think? Don't even get me started with my mom and her accomplishments - we don't have enough pages.

So you must identify your "it" first. Sometimes it is easy to find. Sometimes it takes someone else to identify it for you. Many people I meet have identified their "it." I also meet as many who don't have the slightest idea what their "it" is. We all have something, and most of the time it is obvious.

Don't think for a minute that my only "it" in

life is SM. It is just the one that got my attention so that I would be able to be prepared for the next one and be able to deal with it more effectively.

*Jesus says in **Luke 6:46-49**,*
"Why do you call me, 'Lord, Lord,' and do not do what I say? I will show you what he is like who comes to me and hears my words and puts them into practice. He is like a man building a house, who dug down deep and laid the foundation on rock. When a flood came, the torrent struck that house but could not shake it, because it was well built. But the one who hears my words and does not put them into practice is like a man who built a house on the ground without a foundation. The moment the torrent struck that house, it collapsed and its destruction was complete."

The interesting but sad part of this parable is that if you didn't notice the house that was built on the poor foundation, the destruction there was complete! We can't possibly think that the amount of destruction in relationships, families, businesses, and etc. isn't related to this concept of a proper foundation. Christ, of course is talking about God as being the ultimate foundation point. Let's not forget our community and relationships with those we consider as additional building blocks of our foundation. Quick, who would be the first person you would think of when you are facing a crisis? You have just identified the beginning of your foundation. Sadly, some of us just thought of someone or a group that we have had no contact with in quite some time, but are unintentionally holding out until the storm of life shows up.

Herein lies the beauty of God's promise to us, a love that never ends, takes a vacation, or needs to think about it when we are in need. The problem with this concept or thought process is that it doesn't work to avoid the "it" all together. With the plethora of "its" in our lives, which ones truly derail us? Answer: far too many! Prepare now. God's word teaches us when your "it" shows up big or small, you are already prepared.

This is the whole point of the formula "$F^3 \times G = ?$" avoiding the majority of life's "its" altogether, so that some don't even hit our radar. Why, because we have built this incredible system of dealing with "its," like a great business plan, athletic play, or musical score. It is so well planned, most of the potential problems roll off like water on a duck's back.

FOUNDATION

Lets break this down with the first "F," Foundation. Foundation is simply your relationships and community. You must establish a proper set of relationships with those you trust the

most and who trust in you, but also remember that it is critical that this is not a one-way street. Far too many relationships are built on the one-way principle, that is a network, people who will get you a ways but look out when the "it" in life shows up at your door. The network fades to black, and the real relationships appear. Build relationships and nurture them like a seed in the ground, and they will blossom in to a beautiful garden. Never neglect or take advantage of your foundation.

I've included my foundation plan for you to see. Take a look at it. After you read it, I've included a space in Chapter 9 for you to write out your own.

MY FOUNDATION

God clearly outlines what to do to prepare for the torrents of life. When it comes to these storms, it is not if they come, but when they come! By preparing for this I will have the foundation to withstand anything this life can throw my way. Jesus lays this out perfectly in the Sermon on the Mount, by describing two dwellings, both are struck by storms and only one survives. Which one am I? Or better yet, which one do I want to be?

Luke 6:46-49

"Why do you call me, ' Lord, Lord,' and do not do what I say? I will show you what he is like who comes to me and hears my words and puts them into practice. He is like a man building a house, who dug down deep and laid the foundation on rock. When a flood came, the torrent struck that house but could not shake it, because it was well built. But the one who hears my words and does not put them into practice is like a man who built a house on the ground without a foundation. The moment the torrent struck that house, it collapsed and its destruction was complete."

FOUNDATION CHECKLIST

ATTENDING CHURCH - Am I attending a weekly worship opportunity?

PRAYING - Am I talking and listening to God?

READING MY BIBLE - Am I reading my Bible daily?

GIVING - Am I giving of my finances, time and talent to God's purpose?

BUILDING MY COMMUNITY - Am I sharing of myself in my community (Family, Work, Friends in neighborhood)?

FOUNDATION

FAITH

The second of the three "F's" in the formula is Faith. What and where are you placing your faith? Or maybe whom are you placing your faith in: God, people, your work, money, etc.?

When I first got sick, I found out quickly that I was not going to make it very far by myself. It wasn't that hard to notice; I could barely walk. I was desperate, I needed help. I needed to place my faith in something or someone. You see faith is the belief in something greater than you. God and my family were the primary places I put my faith. Did you know ninety-five percent of Americans say they have a faith in God? Really? Sadly though, for some it is only when that faith is tested that we decide to use it, and when tested with an "it" over our heads. What is our first move? We hit our knees and pray.

There is nothing wrong with the hitting the knees part or faith in your family, friends, coworkers, etc., but once again you can't expect this to work with precision unless first you are tending to it. "Lonely people die lonely." Why? Because they have decided to do it alone. I did that for a while and quickly decided that this approach was deadly and terribly ineffective.

Duke University basketball, under the direction of Coach Mike Krzyzewski, has been one of the most successful college basketball teams in the history of the sport. Why? I believe it is this: faith. In God? No, I think God has more important things to do then worry about whether Duke is winning basketball games. But He (God) is genuinely interested in them in a life-perspective way. The point is that Duke wins more than it loses because of faith in each other. As I stated in a previous chapter, "A good team has faith in

their talent. A great team has faith in each other."
I will take a team with less talent but faith in each
other up against a team with more talent, and I
will win more. When it counts, they will do what is
necessary to accomplish the goal. Talent will just
move on to the next goal. Next I'll share my faith
plan. Write one up in Chapter 9 for your life and
apply it to your formula.

FAITH PLAN

Moses was a person who struggled with identity and was faced with an enormous "i t" freeing his people from pharaoh's grip. God got his attention by speaking to him through a burning bush! That would get my attention! Moses questioned God by asking who shall I say it is that sends me. God's response is timeless and powerful. Simply say: "I Am sends you, I Am who I Am." When we are not able to move, God moves on our behalf w hen you can't, God can w hen you are not able, God says "I Am!"

Do I have faith????

Exodus 3 "The LORD said, "I have indeed seen the misery of my people in Egypt. I have heard them crying out because of their slave drivers, and I am concerned about their suffering. So I have come down to rescue them from the hand of the Egyptians and to bring them up out of that land into a good and spacious land, a land flowing with milk and honey—the home of the Canaanites, Hittites, Amorites, Perizzites, Hivites and Jebusites. And now the cry of the Israelites has reached me, and I have seen the way the Egyptians are oppressing them. So now, go. I am sending you to Pharaoh to bring my people the Israelites out of Egypt." But Moses said to God, "Who am I, that I should go to Pharaoh and bring the Israelites out of Egypt?" And God said,

"I will be with you. And this will be the sign to you that it is I who have sent you: When you have brought the people out of Egypt, you will worship God on this mountain." Moses said to God, "Suppose I go to the Israelites and say to them, 'The God of your fathers has sent me to you,' and they ask me, 'What is his name?' Then what shall I tell them?" God said to Moses, "I am who I am. This is what you are to say to the Israelites: 'I AM has sent me to you.'" God also said to Moses, "Say to the Israelites, 'The Lord, the God of your fathers—the God of Abraham, the God of Isaac and the God of Jacob—has sent me to you.' This is my name forever, the name by which I am to be remembered from generation to generation."

Faith Checklist

Risk - When is the last time I risked something on behalf of God? When is the last time I did something without the fear of the outcome?

Listen - When is the last time I listened to God's prompting?

Action - When is the last time I took action on behalf of God?

Trust - When is the last time I trusted God for something you didn't trust myself for?

Believe - When is the last time I believed when the world said otherwise? I need to take a stand.

FOCUS

The final "F" is focus. We hear a lot about this in life and in sports. Believe me, I have heard my share of this, "C'mon Kuester, focus out there!" When I was diagnosed with SM, one of the biggest problems I had was readjusting my focus. As long as my focus remained on my "it" (SM), I was never going to see the solution, the "mailbox." That was a painful seven-month process, as we discussed in earlier chapters. Some of this pain could have been avoided.

Please understand we all must grieve. No matter what the "it" is, we have to go through a process of healthy and natural grieving. That doesn't mean it goes on forever! We all must move forward, even if it is just a few steps at a time, and focus on the solution. We have all been in the business of pointing out the obvious, something that is wrong. In fact we are all experts

at this life skill. Please change! We need more people with solutions. I like to call these people, "Solutionators," those that seek the solution as they identify a problem. Don't wait until the storms of life hit the shores, be prepared move your focus to the solution, every day. Work on it. Let your walls down and look to solve the problem and move forward. Embrace the small victories, celebrate them, move on, adjust the battle plans, and remember ten steps can turn to twenty.

Here is the way I approach focus. See if it resonates with you. In Chapter 9, we will give you the opportunity to create your own focus plan.

✳ FOCUS PLAN ✳

Throughout scripture God proclaims the premise/promise of focus. If I focus on the "i t" in my life I will lose and my life will become dark. But if my focus remains on God, I will receive life through His gift.

Proverbs 3:5-6 "Tr ust in the LORD with all your heart and lean not on your own understanding; in all your ways acknowledge him, and he will make your paths straight."

Focus Checklist

Watching - What is my visual intake?

Listening - What am I listening to?

Reacting - How am I reacting to things? What is my reaction to events?

Acting - How am I acting toward others? What is my action towards others?

Accountability - Am I allowing others to help me be accountable to God?

GRACE

"G" or Grace is the power juice; it is the opportunity for you to chase after your "mailbox." If you fall, pick yourself up and try again. I know that if I had only attempted my mailbox one time, I never would have made it. The plan wasn't bad, the goal wasn't unattainable; it required patience and effort. Grace is also an opportunity for you to breathe.

In a recent meeting I had with a small business, I suggested to them that they give each other an occasional grace day. Face it; we all aren't on the top of our game all the time. Relax, regroup, and retry; you will find your results will improve. We are such a masked society; we wear this mask during work, this one to another place, and another for something else. With a bit of class and respect, begin taking off your masks. Start being "you" and all God wants you to be. Here is

what grace is not: an excuse to be lazy. It is a free gift. Accept it, and respect it and those who grant it.

Here is my approach to grace for my formula. You'll have an opportunity in Chapter 9 to write out your own.

GRACE PLAN

The beauty of Psalm 63 and Psalm 86: This is what God wants for everyone's life, real life, abundant life... eternal life! That is too hard. But God gave me that gift: Grace – forgiveness through the sacrifice of Jesus. The psalmist reminds me, "O God, you are my God. I will praise you as long as I live." But the part I forget is this: "Teach me your way, O LORD, and I will walk in your truth." God gives me the gift of learning to walk in the ways of the Lord.

Take life moment-by-moment, day-by-day, year-by-year, and God will be faithful just as he was for David "a man after God's own heart." Joy is near. The storms of life are just that, storms, and they will pass. Pursue God and I will find abundant eternal life.

$$F^3 \times G = ?$$

Joy

Success

Happiness

Whatever I want!

Grace Thoughts

Not A Choice - It Is Free...
Unearned Gift From God

Take A "Grace Day!"

Not An Excuse For Poor Choices
Or Behavior

Use It... The Gift Is Yours!

Trust God More, Trust You Less...
More Like Jesus Everyday

$$F^3 \times G = ?$$

Chapter 9 - Applying the Formula

So how do you apply the formula
"$F^3 \times G = ?$" Start with a move any move. Take
an inventory as it relates to your life against the
formula. Where do you stand? What is the status
of your Foundation, Faith and Focus? What result
to you hope to have by applying the formula?
Remember anything is possible in any situation,
I have been living that for the last 15 years and I
don't plan on stopping anytime soon.

We have supplied you with the following blank action plans for you to fill out for yourself. Just like I did I took piece of paper and began to write before I knew it we had a formula. Now it is your turn don't wait, get started today and watch your life take off!

MY FOUNDATION

FOUNDATION CHECKLIST

FAITH PLAN

Faith Checklist

✳ FOCUS PLAN ✳

Focus Checklist

GRACE PLAN

Grace Thoughts

About the Author

Kris Kuester inspires people to change, to overcome, and to rediscover joy in their lives. He currently resides in Atlanta, Georgia, with his wife, daughter, and his daughter's best friend Gracie—a chocolate lab.

In college, Kris was an Academic All-NCC and All North Central Region baseball player at the University of North Dakota, and in his twenties spent five years under the tutelage of Grammy award-winning songwriter and Nashville producer Dennis Morgan. In addition to touring as a successful country music artist, Kris worked with artists like Trisha Yearwood, Marty Stuart, Pam Tillis, and Sawyer Brown, to name a few. But at age thirty, a casual conversation with a physician on a golf course changed his life forever.

In 1996, Kris was diagnosed with syringomyelia, an incurable and neurodegenerative disease of the spinal cord. After two brain surgeries and over that next year, he taught himself how to walk again, how to play his guitar again, and with the Lord's help, he overcame a dark depression.

Kris has been an ordained pastor and gifted worship leader for ten-plus years, and now serves others through his non-profit organization Living With It. Kris says, "You don't have to have a spinal cord disorder like me to be living with something of great consequence that is affecting your daily life in a very personal way. Maybe you've lost a job recently or you're having financial difficulties. Maybe you're sick or someone in your family is sick. Maybe you're struggling with an addiction. What is your 'it'? It could be anything. The good news is that we have been given the tools we need so that we can begin Living With It."

For more information about Living With It Ministries visit our site at www.livingwithit.net.